THE YEAR OF FEARS:

THE 7 MOST IMPORTANT LESSONS I LEARNED THAT WILL SAVE YOU TIME AND MONEY

LYNDA M WEST

Foreword

by Greg S Reid

What a great find you have in front of you in *The Year of Fears*. I know something about manifesting and thinking on a large scale and FEAR is the biggest thing that holds most people back from accomplishing something on a large scale.

Having been published, co-authored and featured in over 60 books, 28 best sellers in 45 countries, five motion pictures, and featured in countless magazines, I continue to share that the most valuable lessons we learn are also the easiest ones to apply. *The Year of Fears* gives practical and easy lessons on how to conquer your fears in order to become a fearless entrepreneur.

When I was personally commissioned by the Napoleon Hill Foundation to interview the most successful people in the world and find out what makes them tick, I embarked on a journey where fear could not get in my way from achieving success. You see, FEAR is what holds us back. FEAR is what keeps us from doing what we want to do. FEAR is the single obstacle that gets us from where we are to where we're going. As a matter of fact, the longest chapter of Napoleon Hill's *Think and Grow Rich* was dedicated to one topic: The Six Ghosts of Fear. Why? Because all of us have fears and it is how we work through those fears that shows who we truly are.

I have worked closely with Lynda West over the past few years and have watched her apply to her everyday life the lessons she learned during her Year of Fears. When I first met her she was timid, but I could instantly see what she had to offer. But she didn't see what she had to offer, so she wasn't putting herself out there. However, once she embarked on her journey, her growth was exponential and now she teaches people all over the world how to conquer their fears so they can live a life of freedom.

I'm honored to be part of her personal and professional growth. As a mentor to many successful entrepreneurs, Lynda ranks at the top of my list as one of the fastest growing individuals I have had the honor to mentor.

With the tools you have in *The Year of Fears*, I encourage you to dream big, to dream differently, and to overcome any obstacles in your life. I know you can and I know that the price of doing so will bring you great joy and the life of freedom you so desire. Once you have mastered fearlessness, your potential will increase tenfold. Or possibly more. I'm not saying that you will not have fears; I am saying that you will learn how to conquer those fears and experience the success that you wish to have.

My advice to you is that you use the tools you now have before you in *The Year of Fears* to stretch your thinking beyond what you ever imagined. Start with big thoughts and build big dreams. Make them real and share them with humanity. You are here to make a difference.

Contents

Staying Connected

I'd love to hear from you. What fears have you had that you've confronted and kicked to the curb? What fears are you still working on? What fears have you not yet addressed?

I love receiving emails with stories from people telling me how they've confronted their fears, so send an email to me at Lynda@LivingLive.tv

Download my free Live Video Content Planner if you're interested in learning how to break through your fear of doing live videos: www.LivingLive.tv/vcp

Schedule a discovery call to see how I can help you work through some of your fears to put you on the path to freedom: www.LivingLive.tv/30

I look forward to hearing from you.

Lynda M West

If you are not Living Live, you are not Living.

p.s. Did I ever tell you about the time I ran away when I was 5 years old and was gone a whole week? Yeah, that's a whole other story.

Abandoning Fear

Have you ever felt stagnant in your life and career? You have all these big ideas and plans that never seem to get executed? And you aren't quite sure why. You look around at other people you consider successful and wonder how they have "made it" and you haven't. You start on projects and dreams, but somewhere along the way you start getting queasy, you think "who am I to have such big dreams?" and "how can I possibly do this?," then you endlessly procrastinate, and soon your dream becomes abandoned on the wayside of your busy life.

If any of that resonated with you, let me assure you that it is all common and 100% fixable. Your body and mind have allowed fear - of success, of failure, of all the bumps in the road - to stop you in your tracks on the road towards success.

I used to feel that way, too, but I don't anymore. The reason? I made one meaningful shift in my approach to life - I decided to stop being scared of fear. Let me repeat that because it is crucial - I decided to stop being scared of fear. I gave myself permission to succeed in spite of my fears.

Fear comes in all different forms and affects our life in so many ways, but when it comes to business endeavors, there are some pretty common gut fears that slow us down, sometimes without our explicit knowledge. They are internalized triggers that keep us from looking at things, listening to things, or moving in the right direction.

When it came to tackling my fear of fear, I committed myself to 365 days of doing something every day that scares me - My Year of Fears. I undertook this process of desensitizing myself to confronting fears. Along the way, I learned some very important lessons and insights, both the power of abandoning fear, and some common-sense protections against disaster in the process. Those are the lessons discussed in this book.

Welcome to a journey that will help you confront your fears and enable you to really live your life and achieve your business dreams on your own terms.

Lesson #1 - Know Your Numbers

When I started my business, I had no idea what the hell I was doing. The most daunting thing to me was the fact that I knew eventually I was going to have to look at "the numbers." I was sure real entrepreneurs knew how much money came in and went out of their businesses down to the penny and carefully followed budgets. I put off looking at my numbers as long as I possibly could and didn't bother with crafting a budget. I'm a visionary, not a numbers cruncher. If you're at all like me, the thought of budgeting makes you want to hurl. You'd rather have a root canal than to work on a budget.

What I didn't want to admit to myself was that my disdain for numbers was actually a masked fear. I was afraid that looking at the financial details of my business would steal my joy.

Blissful Ignorance is Still Ignorance

In 2015, I started my new business. My sister said to me, "You have to create a budget. If you don't create one, you won't know how much money you have to spend and, therefore, you won't know how much you have to make." Now that I put it down in writing it seems so sensible and logical, but I just laughed it off, thinking she was being ridiculous. I had some money set aside to fund my business launch and I was having too much fun as a new entrepreneur to bother with such mundane things as "the numbers."

The summer of 2015 was the summer of following my dreams and passion without being weighed down by the buzzkills of budgets and financial planning. You see, I had been putting on fundraising events for 14 years, but this time I was going to finally put on my dream event, a huge fundraising food festival, the Lemon Zest & Garlic Fest.

The Lemon Zest & Garlic Fest was to be an event like no other event San Diego had ever seen. I would put on an amazing event with garlic and lemon and people would flock to it. We would raise a lot of money for the charity beneficiary, Nsefu Wildlife Conservation Foundation, and I'd make some money for being the masterful creator of this amazing event.

This event was about so much more than money. I had spent the bulk of my adult life doing what others wanted me to do. This time I would decide what I was going to do.

Planning and executing this event was about living the life I wanted to live, being the person I wanted to be, leading a group of people into victory, learning who I was, and what I could do. It would be easy, and the widely successful event would demonstrate to me and the world that quitting my cushy government job six months earlier and selling my childhood home to fund the following of my dreams was a decision of genius.

With so much at stake, you might think I would want to make sure I had a workable budget, but my thoughts were elsewhere. I wanted the event to be what I wanted it to be, how I envisioned it in my head, somewhat like the little girl who always dreamed of her fairytale wedding and now the magical moment was upon her. With all of this lofty (and fun) thought, who wanted to be dragged down with the pedantic exercise of budgeting?

Or maybe it was sheer stubbornness on my part, not wanting to acknowledge that my sister was smarter about something. Whatever the reason, my stubborn refusal to create and follow a budget was a stupid decision. If I had done that, things would have turned out much differently and I would have saved myself tens of thousands of dollars.

It wasn't all about me, though, at least that was the white lie I told myself. This was a charity event and I wanted to give a lot of money to the charity. I made a commitment to myself and to the charity that I was going to donate money no matter what.

I hoped that donation would come from proceeds out of the event instead of my own pocket, but I replaced a budgeting process with wishful thinking. I truly believed deep in my soul that everything was going to work out and that we were at least going to break even.

Now, be honest. You've done that, too. You are so excited about what your business is doing, you have the proverbial faith that can move mountains that you are doing the right thing, and you don't have a budget either. No judgment here, I assure you; I get it.

I gave myself four months to put on this huge event where I was hoping to have 1,000 people in attendance. I needed to bring in revenue through sponsorships, vendors, and ticket sales. I had expenditures for marketing and a hundred other things. A set percentage of profits were allocated for the chosen charity. A financially successful event would have more revenue than expenditures, obviously.

Halfway through planning the event, I was gushing to my sister about how much fun I was having planning this awesome event and how so many people were excited to attend. She supported my joy, but also tried to tie it back to reality. As she had done when I first started my new business, she said, "Let me see your budget."

I was a little irritated, I'll admit, and responded, "I don't have a budget and I don't want to create one." She laughed at me. I was adamant that I was not going to prepare a budget. I was so pig-headed about it because I was having more fun than I'd ever had in my life. I didn't want a pesky budget to take away my joy.

A week later I saw her again and she said to me, yet AGAIN, "Let me see your budget." And, again, I told her "I don't have one." I hadn't prepared a budget and had no idea how much money I had already spent and how much more money I was going to spend and, therefore, had no idea how much money I needed to bring in.

This time, she wouldn't accept my answer and forced me to sit down with her and create a budget. Mind you, this was halfway through the process; the event was to take place in less than two months and a lot of money had already come and gone (mostly gone) by that point.

My sister forced me to sit down with her and answer all of her questions related to the event and the money. I was so thankful and relieved to know where I stood financially. We agreed that we would look at the budget every other week so that we could see the numbers to discover what we needed to tweak so I would make money instead of lose money.

I didn't look at my budget, though. My old patterns crept back in and we didn't meet to go over the budget simply because I didn't want to look at the numbers. I loved being ignorant in this situation. I was happy being ignorant. There was another reason, too. I knew why I didn't want to look at the numbers. It was because I was losing a lot of money.

As our bank account continued to quickly drop with no revenue coming in, instead of me saying "let's course-correct and do something different," I, instead, said, "Let's keep going. This is what I want to do." Every time I felt like I was losing money, I felt driven to do more so that there would be something to give to the charity at the end of the event. I pretended that positive intent would overcome everything else. It turned into "budgeting" by emotion, not the numbers.

As the big day approached, I was so excited! What an amazing event it would be on a sunny July day in gorgeous Southern California. But life does not always comply with our dreams, and, as a particular slap in the face, I discovered that songwriters who claim "it never rains in Southern California" were lying.

On this particular July day, it rained more than it has ever rained in San Diego's history. There was thunder and lightning and flooding, three hours of rain with tents collapsing, no music for fear of electrocution, and no TV coverage because it was pouring down rain. The Sheriff's Department almost shut down our Beer Garden and 700 attendees walked around looking like wet rats.

I'll confess, my first flitting concern about the numbers did go through my brain as soon as I realized we were going to be in the middle of a massive rainstorm. I wondered whether I should close down the event, but quickly realized that wasn't an option. I couldn't close down the event because I had invested so much money into it (I didn't know how much, of course, but I knew it was a lot) and I didn't really have that kind of money to throw away. I would have to refund everyone because (another mistake I made) I didn't have a "rain or shine" clause when I sold the tickets. I had already lost a lot of money, but closing down the event would have made it a financial bloodbath. With the lightning, though, it was a potentially dangerous situation. Dang! It was so hard to decide what to do.

But I quickly brushed aside my concerns and determined that no amount of rain was going to steal my joy. I chose to make the most of it and have as much fun as possible, and everybody else seemed to be having a great time, too. It was the worst storm in San Diego's history and people were enjoying themselves. It was comical, crazy, and potentially dangerous, but we had a great time just the same. I engaged in my favorite fallback position of ignorant bliss, at least for the day.

Now I could stop this story right here and say "look, a positive attitude conquers all," but that wouldn't be the whole story. I could also say that what I learned in four months would have taken me four years to learn in school and would have cost me more money, but that isn't the whole story either. My mom always said, "Ignorance is bliss." Well, it has its time and place, but when running a business "ignorance is ignorance." Ignoring a budget for the maiden voyage of my new business ended up being one of the dumbest and most costly things I have ever done.

As the rain tapered off and the revelers wandered home, the enormity of the situation began to sink in. I finally had to sit down and look at the numbers and get a more realistic picture of my dream event. Turns out it wasn't just the wet attendees that got soaked; my husband and I lost $70,000 on the event. I had spent four months planning an event that was a financial flop. It was a terribly costly lesson learned, especially when I realized that it was avoidable if only I had prioritized my business budget over my ignorant joy. Joy is great, wonderful, in fact, but concurrent ignorance has a heavy price tag.

What I know now is that although I could not have predicted the freak rainstorm, I could have been prepared to immediately understand its implications, make an immediate informed decision on whether or not to postpone the event, and take preemptive steps to mitigate any loss from unforeseen contingencies for a large outdoor event. All that stress I could have saved myself and my husband if only I had a put together a budget up front and followed it.

Numbers Don't Lie

Numbers don't lie because they do not fall prey to the allure of chasing one's joy. Avoiding the truth doesn't immunize yourself from the consequences of the numbers. Money lost is still lost. Bills due are still due. And eventually your business will die from lack of financial health.

If you have no idea how much it costs to run your business, then you will have no idea how much you need to make. If you have no idea how much money you need to make, then you have no idea how many clients you need or how much to charge for your services or how many products you need to sell. That sounds obvious, but it is the simple truth.

Think of your business budget somewhat like a household budget. Let's say you have an income of $4,000 every month from your job and you have expenses of $4,200 every month. You are short $200 every month. You know you are short $200 every month, so you know you have to do something to make an extra $200 so that you don't go into negative income. If you don't make that extra $200, you risk getting your electricity turned off or your TV turned off or losing your cell phone or not having enough money for gas to get you to and from work. If you find yourself short every month for your household income and expenses, then it is very important for you to create a personal budget so that you can see where you can cut back or see how much more money you need to make in order to be able to continue the lifestyle you currently have.

Now, I realize that in the back of your mind you are thinking about businesses like Facebook and Amazon that operated for years without ever making a profit and look where they are now. Well, if you have that kind of financial backing, millions of investment dollars to spend to build your business before anyone expects you to turn a profit, congratulations and I'm jealous. But you are still going to need a budget and know where your money comes from and goes to, you'll just have more flexibility for errors.

If you want to create a life of abundance, you need to make sure you have a surplus. If you want to remove lots of stress from your life, create your business budget such that it leaves both room for unexpected expenses, and leaves a surplus. Be conservative on your estimates of income and somewhat exaggerate your expense estimates.

It's important to have a baseline of expectations to serve as your constant in the midst of, at least initially, wildly fluctuating income from month to month. This should level out as your business develops, but learning to live with the ups and downs from the beginning is best. What happens a lot of times for beginning business owners is that they are not used to having extra money some months and they end up immediately finding a way to spend it on something outside of the budget, instead of leaving it as a surplus to help stabilize their business finances.

Have you ever heard the stories about people winning the lottery and then spending all of the money within a year or two? Do you know why this happens? They don't have a budget either. It just feels like so much money that they are sure they will never run out of it, and that's why they do.

Money has a weird energy. When we suddenly have money and we weren't used to having money we don't know what to do with it. The lottery winners are thrust into a life of spending that they never had before. They don't know how to handle it. The reason they don't know how to handle it is because they've never experienced it. This happens not only to lottery winners, but to sports stars, movie stars, you name it, and it will happen to you too as a business owner. There is something called money mindset. In order to know how to handle money, your mind has to be ready to handle the money, and a budget is a concrete way to prepare yourself.

If you come from a money mindset where you don't have much money or you didn't grow up with a lot of money, when your business starts making money, you are not going to know how to handle it. That is why it is so important to budget. When you see how much money is coming in and going out, it is easier to make decisions based on the facts.

Lesson #2 - Define Your Own Success

I'll bet you didn't know that more people fear success than they fear failure. They are afraid of doing the things they want to do, even sometimes the things they feel called to do, because they never owned their own definition of "success." What does success mean for you? Every person's success is different. You have to decide what being successful is and then you have to put yourself on a path to attaining that success by doing whatever it takes for you to achieve it. Success comes in many forms.

"Thank God! The bastard is dead" were the first words out of my mom's mouth when my dad took his last breath. Imagine that. My mom felt trapped by my dad and to ensure that she would not take the brunt of his anger she lived her entire life for him. Because of that, when he took his last breath, she could finally take her first breath of her new life. Sadly, her new chapter in life was cut short a few years later by cancer. I wept for my mom. At that very moment I decided I was going to live my life to its fullest.

I decided many years ago that I would spend as much of my life as possible doing things that I love and surrounding myself with positive and uplifting people who want to make a huge impact on the world. For me, that is success. It originally had nothing to do with finances, but after my ill-adventured, budget-less Lemon Zest & Garlic Fest, I have added to my success equation having enough money to continue pursuing my positive, uplifting other things.

At different stages of my life, success has meant something different. When I was younger, success meant landing the boyfriend I wanted. All I could think about was this one boy (his name was Greg) and how I was going to get him to like me and to become my boyfriend. I focused on that for a period of time and, finally, he became my boyfriend. Yes, I had success!

When I got older, success came in different forms, like, for example, buying the car that I wanted. I had to save enough money to buy that car and, after several months, I finally had enough money for a down payment and was able to get a car loan to get the dream car that I had wanted for so long. Yes, I had success!

Those are simple successes compared to large company successes. The idea of success to me now is completely different than what my idea of success was back then. I realize, now, that the success that I want has nothing to do with just me; it has to do with other people and will involve a team. My mission is to help 5.5 million women entrepreneurs grow their business through education and training. It's bold and brash, but what benefit is there in thinking small?

What Do You Want Our of Your Life?

What does success mean for you? What does a fulfilled life look like to you? Everyone has a different idea of success, so you need to decide what success means to you. Is your idea of success employing people and providing jobs for others or is it where you don't have to work a 9 to 5, but work for yourself where you call all the shots?

Every person's answer is going to be different. You have to decide what being successful is, what a fulfilled life looks like, and then you have to put yourself on a path to attaining that success. You get to promise yourself to do whatever it takes for you to achieve your success.

Success comes in many forms. You need to know what success means to you and you have to go after it. Had my mom known what success meant to her, it's possible she would have taken different routes in her life and been happier. I spent much time with my mom her last three years and learned a lot from her. One of the things I did learn is that I want to make sure that when I take my last breath that I did everything I wanted to do. That includes remaining focused on what it is I want to do so that I can live a happy and successful life.

For me, happiness equals success. But I have a few more concrete goals, too. For example, I want to be a talk show host. Okay, I said it out loud. I remember the first time I actually said that I wanted to be a talk show host and I told somebody that I wanted to be just like Ellen DeGeneres. What I actually said was, "I am going to be San Diego's Ellen DeGeneres." The first time I said that it sounded weird to me, pretentious even, but as I started saying it more often it was becoming real and I knew then that I had to start putting things into action to make it happen.

I see myself hosting an online talk show. I see it so clearly that I'm currently on the road to creating my talk show. By the time you are reading this book, I may already have that show. I just know it because the vision is so clear.

It's such an exciting feeling to say I want to do that and then to follow the dream and passion and then to put it into action. Will it be successful? I have no doubt that it will. How can I have such confidence that it will be successful?

Well, I not only have defined what success looks like to me, but I have formulated specific goals, developed a prototype of my ideal clients, implement time management skills, seek counsel from others along the way, and surround myself with positivity, all things I will be discussing in this book.

When you are defining your success, however, don't get pulled into the trap of comparing your dreams and outcomes with others. That can take an unnecessary toll on your mind and distract from the plan that will get you, and only you, to your goals.

When I first thought about doing the talk show, I started comparing myself to Ellen. What had been her path to success? How could I follow in her footsteps. Now that I think it through, that method of seeking my own success was absolutely ridiculous. Ellen has been in front of audiences for many years. She started off by doing stand-up comedy and building an audience. I haven't done any of that. How can I possibly compare myself to her? I can't, but that doesn't mean that I can't have my own talk show. I just need to get there through a different path and build off of my own skills and abilities, connections, and opportunities.

Comparing yourself to others where they are today and from where you are today is a pointless exercise. They took a totally different route than you did with your life and may have gotten an earlier start than you. It is much smarter to look at what the person is doing now, look at how they got there for informational purposes, then plot out your own path that will get you to the same destination.

Don't hesitate to even reach out to that person whose position you admire and seek and ask them how they did it. Ask about the bumps and bruises they had along the way that can prevent you from encountering the same bumps and bruises. You might be surprised how often people will be happy to help you out (and worst case, they just won't respond to you). It's time to turn your dreams into your reality.

Discover Who You Are

The first step to defining your own success story is to stop comparing your goals and journey to that of others. Take the time and spend your energy discovering who you are.

It was August 2014 when it hit me that there HAS to be more to life than what I was doing. I decided it was time for me to discover who I am. I signed up with a life coach who could help me figure it all out. She helped me embark on the most transformative five months of my life. I went from somebody who didn't have any direction at all, and didn't have any idea who I was, to somebody who started to exude confidence and recognize the excellence within me. It's always been there, but I never knew it because I never wanted to look at it. When was the last time you looked for excellence within you? Trust me, it's there.

Like me, you have the option of focusing on what you have not done for your whole prior life, or you can look at what you can do. Until your dying breath, you still have a chance to transform your life in the direction you want it to take. Blame -- of yourself, of others, of your circumstances -- is a waste of precious time.

Is it hard work to discover yourself? Yeah. My first, and really only, job was to become aware of myself and my surroundings. I had to be aware of everything going on in my life every single day and how that felt. I had to become aware of how I reacted to situations around me and how that felt. Then I had to decide whether I wanted to change my reactions for future or not. It is the same process for everyone, whether you have an insightful life coach or try to do it alone.

What's really cool about discovering who you are is that if you discover that you don't like who you are you can change that. It is in your control to change who you are and who you are being. One thing I discovered along this journey was that it was time for me to be brave and share my weaknesses, for in my weaknesses others saw my strengths.

I discovered the power of weakness when I started a weight loss journey and shared it all on Facebook. Although I was scared to post my pictures because I was the heaviest I had ever been, I felt that if I posted my pictures it would hold me accountable and I would lose the weight. The result was way better than I expected. People were telling me how brave I was to share those pictures. I didn't feel brave at all. In fact, showing my weakness made me feel even more vulnerable. It was crazy. My weakness (in the face of mint chocolate chip ice cream, among other things) was what had caused me to gain so much weight in the first place.

Now, people were saying how brave I was while I was showing my weakness. I had turned the tables on one weakness to find strength and bravery on the other side.

THE YEAR OF FEARS

A lot of people are too scared to put themselves out there in a way that shows how weak they are. We are not taught to be that way. We are taught to hide our vulnerabilities, to never show fear. Turns out that all of that was wrong. Sharing my weaknesses, showing my vulnerability and authentic self, gave me strength I never knew I had. I am no longer scared to show who I really am and that freedom has propelled my business life like nothing else. Freedom from fear is the most amazing thing!

Throughout this journey of discovering who I am, things changed on an almost daily basis. Step by step I found myself changing from somebody I really didn't like into somebody I wanted to be. So many factors helped me with my change, but strategic social media use really put me on a bullet train to growth. Posting about myself on social media really helped me become more clear on a daily basis. After five months people were telling me that I was a totally different person than I had been just five months earlier. They were right.

The first thing to do to start your journey of discovering who you are is to look at who you really want to be. That might sound counter-intuitive, but really part of discovering who you are is discovering who you want to be.

Being on the journey to self-discovery can be scary at times, but it can also be very thrilling. Some of the exercises my life coach had me do really opened the door to my self-discovery. Here is one of them. Make a list of five people that you really like. Call each of them and ask them, "When I walk into a room, what shows up?" Then write down everything they say. You don't speak at all. At all. Then when they are done saying what they say, you ask them one simple question, "Is that all?" Sometimes they will say more and sometimes they will say, "Yes, that's all." After they are done, you simply thank them and hang up the phone. Don't have a full-on conversation with them. Just end the conversation as it is. You are going to have a lot of confused friends (you can fill them in on the details later), but you are also going to have great insight into who you are and what you are putting out into the world.

This one exercise was one of the most valuable exercises I did with my life coach. Some of the responses were so enlightening and also helped me discover that I'm a much better person than I ever gave myself credit for. It put me on the road to discovering that thinking highly of yourself is not a bad thing, but, on the contrary, is a very important part to self-growth and to stepping into the excellence of who you are.

Step Into Your Excellence

Now that you're discovering who you are and who you really want to be, it's time to step into that excellence and become who you want to become. I will use my Ellen DeGeneres example to share an illustration of what I started doing. I said to myself, "Here I am today being the person I am today, but I want to be like Ellen DeGeneres." I wanted to do what she is doing. So I started doing some research and discovering what she did to get where she is. Well, she has a 30-year jump on me, so I can't take the same amount of time as she took to get there (because I'd be 84 before I accomplish what she's accomplished). I can, however, do something slightly different and use the stepping stones available to me, so that I'm doing something similar to Ellen, something that will fulfill my hopes and desires and help the people I want to help.

I've often said that I can do what Ellen does because I can dance and I can interview people and I can give away prizes. I just don't have her size of audience. I have to start somewhere, and that is what I am already doing.

I started down that path by doing something similar to her. She dances and I love to sing, so January 1, 2016, I decided to sing Happy Birthday to all of my Facebook friends. I've been doing it every day since then. It's been really awesome because every day I have an opportunity to sing Happy Birthday and bring joy to people's lives. I've actually had some people private message me to tell me that I was the only person who wished them Happy Birthday. Those messages are what keeps me going every day. I absolutely love it. It's so much fun. On occasion I will have friends sing along with me and they really have a good time doing it, too. So that takes care of the dancing part.

The next part is to interview people. Well, in 2017 I decided to start interviewing people on my Facebook page. At first I was interviewing random people, but then I started having more of a focus and decided I was going to interview business people who can help businesses grow. I would bring them on and they would share their knowledge with my audience and it gave me an opportunity to do two things: I was able to bring experts from different fields and share them with my audience and was able to give exposure for those experts to a new group of people. I see this as a win, win, win. The audience wins, the expert wins, I win.

So the next step is for me to give away cool prizes. That ball is in motion. I'm working on sponsorships and am really excited to start offering prizes to people who are watching the show. This plan has been in motion for about two years and it's finally starting to gain some steam.

Ellen has four books published. You have my first one in your hands right now. Send me your email and I'll let you know when books #2, #3, and #4 come out.

As far as stepping into my excellence, what I did is I took something that I really love and figured out how I could put that thing into action and make it my own. My business, Living Live, is the platform that enables me to do this.

Now it's your turn. Make a list of everything you love doing. Your list can include washing a dog, playing video games, hiking, hanging out with people, etc. Whatever it is that you absolutely love doing and know you could spend a lot of hours doing, write it down.

This might take you a couple weeks to come up with your entire list, but get started today. Get started right now. Write them out on the last page of this chapter.

Then I want you to take that list of all the things that you absolutely love doing and I want you to figure out what the commonality is between them, then figure out what is one thing that you can do that incorporates most, if not all, of them.

When I made my list, I came up with something that really surprised me. I am a coach and mentor. I have been mentoring and coaching people most of my life, but I never thought of myself that way. I coach people through their fears so they can accomplish goals they never thought possible. It's so rewarding and I love it. There are so many other things that I love doing, too, but that is my main focus. This is really what freedom is all about.

When you discover that one thing that really lights you up, it's time for you to tackle it, put it into motion and make it a huge part of your life. Don't let anybody stop you from fulfilling your dreams or your wishes. Don't let anybody get in your way.

Life is too short to spend it worrying about other people or living it for other people. There are too many people who live their life for others at the expense of their own unique worth and possible contribution to the world at large. When they get to the end of their life, they spent a lot of time wishing they hadn't sold themselves short. My wish for you is that you'll take some of this information and discover who you are and use that excellence to live the life you want to live, the life you're supposed to live, the life you were meant to live. Are you on board? I sure hope so.

LIST OF 20 THINGS I LOVE DOING

_____

_____

_____

_____

_____

_____

_____

_____

_____

_____

_____

_____

_____

_____

Be YOU!!!

You spent some time discovering who you are and who you want to become. Now it's time to start living that life. How do you do that? Well, you start putting yourself out there as the person you are and as you become the person you want to become you continue to put out the person you are at that time. That sounds a little confusing, but what I mean is that as long as you are putting yourself out there as who you are right this moment, then you are on the right track.

Being authentic is something so many people are scared to be because they are fearful that people will judge them for who they are. However, if you think about it, does that really matter? They may be already judging the fake you; so what if they also judge the real you? That's on them and the less you worry about their opinion, the farther you will go in life.

People who are critical of others are also overly critical of themselves. This might be you now, but it doesn't have to be you from now on. I know this all too well because that used to be me. I would look at magazines and criticize the movie stars and celebrities. I would watch TV and criticize everybody on it. I would see somebody walking by in a very fancy suit and I would criticize them. Who do they think they are? That was the question that was always in my mind. I don't know why my thoughts always seemed to go in that direction, but it really doesn't matter anymore. I committed to change it. More accurately, as I started being authentic and knowing who I wanted to become, I started spending my time practicing becoming the person I wanted to become. I no longer had any need or desire to be critical of others; I had better and more fun things to do.

People who are in the spotlight probably really put themselves out there in life, took risks of being seen and heard, and I can appreciate that now. My hope for them is that they are very happy with their life, love what they are doing, and are living the life they want to live.

Authenticity is something that is not practiced often enough. Once you start living your life authentically, you will start attracting to you people who are just like who you really are. If you are being inauthentic, you will attract to you people who are like your inauthentic self.

This is why being authentic is such a crucial part of living.

Once I started living my life authentically, I discovered that people I did not want to be around started disappearing from my life and my life is richer for it. No matter how scary it may sound to share with people who you really are, or to claim your own version of success and fulfillment, I highly recommend taking the steps to do it starting right now.

Lesson #3 - Focus on One Path

Once you let go of the shackles of fear and embrace the fullness of life, you might go a little crazy as you explore every option, every path not previously taken. That's great, but not a sustainable path to your successful future.

After working in the corporate world the majority of my life, at the age of 51 I decided to leave my job. I was going to follow my passion of "helping people." My life coach pushed me for more specification. "Maybe you need to figure out what that means so that you can have a clear path to follow."

I heard her, but I didn't listen. I left my corporate job and immediately embarked on nine different paths. All of them involved "helping people," but none could possibly be successful until I narrowed my focus.

Imagine driving and coming to a stop sign at one of those crazy intersections with like five different streets you can turn on. Trying to take every street is unlikely to get you to your destination, even more so when you are unclear what your destination actually is. Without a proven path, you can get lost. Without selecting a path, you'll just go around in circles.

The same is true with your business. If you don't choose a path or a defined destination, you could end up lost and flailing around like I did for so long.

When I left my corporate job in November of 2014, I came out of the gate with so many ideas and instead of taking the time to pick one or two to pursue in a defined fashion, I just pursued them all. I was acting like a child on her first trip to Disneyland trying to check out all of the rides at the same time, with cotton candy in one hand and a big stuffed bear in the other. I had no focus and had no goals except to help people, and have fun doing it. I really confused everyone, even myself. Because I had not put my plans into focus, how could I expect those around me to know what on earth I was doing? How could anyone sign up to be a client or recommend my services to others when even I didn't know what I was really doing.

For a while, I confused busyness with focus, much like the cartoon character Tasmanian Devil who is a whirlwind of noise. Every once in a while, he will stop to look at something, and then goes back to his devilish spinning out of control. Had I spent a little more time stopping from my similar spinning out of control, I would have sooner found the focus I needed to succeed.

I used to think that the busier I was the more I was getting done. Nothing could be further from the truth. I remember my mom saying, "The hurrieder I go the behinder I get." It never made any sense to me when she said it, but I now finally understand what she meant. Spinning wheels is not the same as forward motion, it just makes you dizzy.

The more out of control your life appears to be, the more out of control your life is. You may not be the best judge of this. Ask friends and family members what they see. Are you constantly frantically running from project to project, or are you calmly progressing from one step to the next in business development? When was the last time you stopped to focus on anything?

There's a saying that as an entrepreneur you want to build the plane while you're flying it. While there is truth to that adage, trying to build a plane and a helicopter at the same time while flying pushes that exercise too far and you are bound to crash.

While you are living in chaos, it is impossible to create. Creation happens during silence, creating a plan of action for building your business included. If you take time to slow down your world and step away from all the noise, creation and focus will happen. You must trust that it will happen because there will be blank space in your head that can be filled in. Slow down to speed up.

Follow One Course Until Successful

There have been times during my life that so much was going on that I didn't take time to slow down to allow for that necessary creative space. I was too busy to notice its absence. Then, one day, my business coach asked me a very simple question, "What are you focusing on?" My response surprised even me, as I explained that I was focusing on this and that and this and that. I was "focusing" on about four different projects. He smiled and shared a bit of genius with me. F.O.C.U.S. is an acronym for "Follow One Course Until Successful." He told me I needed to make a decision of what I wanted to do and then to focus on that one thing. I needed to make a decision on one thing, one project, and follow through on it. I needed to stop everything else. It didn't mean stopping the rest forever, but meant stopping the rest at least temporarily so that I could be successful on one project. Once I became successful on that one project, then I could add one more thing. OMG! It made total sense. Yay! Finally!

"Follow One Course Until Successful" has stuck with me ever since. I now see how important it is to slow down so that I could speed up my business development. Doing a lot of things at the same time just consumes energy, it doesn't always equate with forward momentum.

Following one course until you are successful is one of the key elements to getting you on the right track to achieving the success you want to achieve. Focus is a requirement to attain success. Many of today's leaders and industry professionals have spent over 10,000 hours working on one particular task in order to become successful at it. For example, people who are in the Olympics practice their craft thousands and thousands of hours. Basketball players, football players, soccer players, musicians, artists, the list goes on, practice their craft over and over and over and over again and again. Imagine if they had split their time between multiple endeavors, spending only 1,000 hours on any one thing.

Hone in on the craft that you want to be successful doing. Spend as much time as possible focusing on that one thing. If you spend most of your energy perfecting what it is you want to be successful at, successful will come.

How many people do you know who are business owners who own a lot of different businesses? There are a lot of them out there. But I bet the successful ones are the ones who started with one business and became successful at it before they added another business.

Another common scenario of split focus is people who are both trying to work a job and start a business on the side. Sometimes you need a job to provide income to support a new business, but you still need to select your focus. If your job is a means to an end, a steady income to keep a roof over your head while you build your business, make sure it doesn't compete. Be clear about the amount of time and energy you are committing to the job, being fair to your employer, but be just as clear about your commitment to your business.

Go Farther Faster With Focus

Just like momentum, focus will help you to build speed faster because you are narrowly focused on one thing and are concentrating on how to achieve that one, so everything you do is geared toward that one thing. When you go out networking, you talk about that one business. When you get on the phone and talk to people, you talk about that one business. When you talk to a potential client, you talk about that one business and what it can do for that client. Everything you do is related to that one business. You are so focused and ready to take over the world. Your focus is going to lead to your success.

Are you doing more than one thing? Are you trying to be successful in more than one area? If your focus is split into two, three, four different areas, you may eventually become successful, but it will be much slower and harder. Even if you are a great multitasker, your brain still has to split its thoughts and energies.

Just because I finally understood the concept of focus doesn't mean it was easy to confine myself to one project at a time. To make a decision on what my first area of focus would be, I had to weigh out my options and make a decision and, yes, I was going to have to stop working on some things that were fun. I wouldn't have had four projects going at one time if I didn't enjoy what I was doing, and cutting three of those out of my life (at least for now) felt like a reduction of my joy. I also enjoyed the butterfly life of flitting from project to project and didn't want to confine myself to one flower at a time, so to speak. But it had to be done.

It took me two weeks of going back and forth from one idea to another to decide which projects I was going to give up in order to follow one course. It was a crazy process. Each time I decided on one thing, something came up and I changed my mind back to the other thing. For two weeks I felt like a ping-pong ball, flipping back and forth in indecision.

In the end, my coach and I finally found a way to incorporate much of what I loved doing into one business idea. I felt a little bit like I was using a loophole to the F.O.C.U.S. mantra, but was intrigued with our new plan of incorporating everything I love doing into one comprehensive business model.

Until I had discovered my one business idea and focused on it, I was a spiral of confusion for myself and others. If you confuse potential clients, they will not buy from you. Discovering my focus meant I knew how to communicate when I was networking or posting on social media. Having focus meant I would no longer confuse my potential clients.

Here's how I figured out what to focus on. I wrote a list of all of the things I absolutely love doing. Then I looked at my list and figured out how I can incorporate all of those into one business idea. Then the magic started happening. The stars started to align. Eureka! I found it.

If you know what you love doing, I recommend sitting down and figuring out what the commonality is to all those things and start doing that more frequently, just like we talked about in Chapter 2. It's that important.

Lesson #4 - Focus on Ideal Client

"Be careful what you wish for, for you will surely get it" is a phrase often reflecting wishing for something unhelpful in life, something you really didn't want after all. But how about if you are utilizing your newfound fearlessness to actually wish for what you really want, and what you really want in abundance? How might that look? Pretty good, actually, especially when it comes to picking your ideal client.

Focusing on your goals will, sooner or later, require you to identify who you want to impact with your business. When I first embarked on my entrepreneurial journey, people would ask me, "Who is your target market?" or "Who is your ideal client?" and I'd say, "My what?" It didn't take long, however, for me to get focused on developing my target market, an "ideal client" who embodied the characteristics of clients I was hoping to attract.

In order to sell, whether its products or services, you need to know to whom you are going to sell and for whom your products or services are a fit. Because of the nature of my business - consulting - a target market is less important than an ideal client. Here's why.

If your business sells products or services of an arm's-length basis (selling widgets through retailers), your ideal end customer is going to be someone whose needs are going to be fulfilled by your product and you market directly to them. It doesn't matter if you "like" your ideal customer or not, as long as you "know" them well. However, if your business is as a consultant or other direct service provider, you will soon realize that your ideal client is not as much about the person you serve as it is about the person you work with. If you are going to be spending hours each week working with your ideal client, you want people you will like being around and who will like being around you.

Identifying your ideal client is an ongoing process. When I first started my business I thought I wanted to work with people who are working in corporate jobs who didn't want to be there anymore, but didn't know how to leave because they didn't know what they were going to do if they left their job. I figured I could empower them, guide them, and send them on their way to a prosperous future. That was my target market for about six months.

Turns out, it wasn't quite that simple. Just because you are unhappy with your current job, that doesn't mean you are willing to do what it takes to get out and launch a new, successful career. I could cajole, encourage, and try to lead the way to change, but some people, despite the best coaching, are just too scared to leave their job and they won't do it.

I needed to refine my ideal client parameters. I wanted to work with people who are uplifting and motivated and want to achieve success. I wanted to work with people who didn't spend time coming up with excuses as to why they weren't achieving their success, but would instead learn, plan, pivot, work hard, repeat until it works. That's who I wanted to work with, people who would just say, "Okay, I'll do that" and then they would do it and become successful.

One of my clients, Amanda, personified my ideal client. I was able to help her in a big way because I would make recommendation after recommendation and she would take those recommendations and just do them. After only one year, she increased her revenue by more than 400%! I remember the day she came to me and she said, "For the first time in 7 years I am off of government aid. For the first time since my boys have been born I was able to enroll them in summer camp programs. I have money and I don't stress over money all the time anymore. I remember just a year ago when I would get so stressed out about anything related to money and now I don't." Those are the success stories I work to create for my clients every day, and Amanda has become my ideal client prototype.

I know what you are thinking right now (well, at least some of you). Isn't looking for an ideal client something you do after you already have a bunch of clients? "Beggars cannot be choosers" is a phrase that often comes to mind for beginning business owners. You are so desperate for clients, so desperate for income, that you are willing to take anyone and anything, promising yourself that you can get picky later on. Let me assure you, business doesn't work that way. If you can get clear on your ideal client up front, you will save yourself a great deal of time, energy, and money.

I'm going to show you some tips that are going to help you save time, money and energy just by being clear on your ideal client.

Marketing to the Wrong People is a Waste of Time, Energy and Money

Every dollar you spend on marketing should be a dollar that is used to talk to the people that you want to work with. Marketing includes ads, social media, mailers, networking events, etc. I've heard business owners say they help "anybody who has skin," which is just a variant on the "beggars cannot be choosers" concept. Well, if you think about that, that is absolutely ludicrous. A baby has skin and so does an 80-year-old, but their skin is not the same and doesn't have the same needs.

It will cost a lot of marketing dollars to market to "anyone who has skin." Every marketing dollar would be spread amongst billions of people. However, by narrowing the actual target market to, say, women aged 45 who have two kids who are out of the house, are married, love to travel, have a grandchild who lives in a different state, who works a 9 to 5 as a receptionist, and is getting ready to retire, marketing dollars can be much more useful. Every dollar in marketing expense can be directed to where those ideal clients spend their time and make purchase decisions, and your marketing dollars will stretch so much further than if by targeting "anybody who has skin."

If you don't know who your ideal client is, all of your marketing is going to be blindly directed to people who aren't interested in what you have to offer or those you aren't interested in working with.

Here's one of many examples: Hallmark cards. They have determined that their target market is women ages 25 to 54. Therefore, they do not spend any marketing dollars targeted to men, children, or women outside of that age range because that would be a waste (or at least less than optimum use) of their time, effort, energy and money. They may even go to deeper levels of targeting by knowing where their ideal/target customers live, what kind of movies she watches, if she has kids, if she is married or single, what kind of food she eats, or a myriad of other factors.

How can businesses know all of this detail? Well, there are many sources for that information and social media platforms have gotten very effective in collecting and disseminating it. Facebook is one of the fastest growing marketing platforms out there. Facebook may have started because these guys wanted to pick up chicks at school, but at some point they started monetizing it, not by charging users, but by collecting data about users for marketers to use (and by making quizzes and addictive games on the platform). Facebook is one of the fastest growing marketing platforms out there because they both recognized and capitalized on the concept of the ideal client.

Think about it, how many times have you responded to a quiz on Facebook, testing whether you are a "real Alaskan" or something by answering questions about your knowledge and preference for things? And these aren't one-off activities. Their games are addictive, inducing people to spend hours and hours a day on the platform, making themselves available to see marketing ads, marketing targeted just to your preferences and interests.

I'll admit, I got sucked into that addictive marketing vortex once upon a time. Facebook had this cool game called Farmville (it might still be out there, but I am staying clear of it). I played it, my friends played it, my mom played it. At one point I found myself spending anywhere from 5 to 7 hours a day farming my virtual farms. During those hours I was both giving Facebook more information about myself, my habits, my preferences, and was being marketed to by savvy businesses who knew what I was most likely to buy, including other addictive games. (In case you are wondering, I finally recognized the impact this addiction was having on the rest of my life and stopped cold turkey. Perhaps if I had read Chapter 5 about time management, I would have quit sooner.)

Facebook has been able to use their algorithms to find people who like certain things or topics and are able to target those specific people to sell them a product or service. Why? Because they also understand that targeted marketing gets the highest levels of return for your marketing dollars.

Clear Messages Attract Better Clients

Knowing your ideal client not only helps you spend your marketing dollars more efficiently, but it also helps you refine your marketing message. The clearer your message, the easier it is to attract clients to you.

What exactly does your business do? Are you describing it to others in a way that induces people to say "I want that!" Your friends and family have heard you talk about your business, right? Go and ask them what they understand your business to be. If they have a hard time telling you what you do, then you haven't been explaining it correctly. It's as simple as that.

Make sure you check your ego at the door before doing this exercise so that when you talk to people about what you do, and ask them to explain what you do, that you don't get defensive. Don't let your ego get in the way of your growth. Open your mind, open your heart, open your brain to learning as much as you possibly can by listening more than speaking. This is a good exercise to practice anyway, but especially when you're trying to get clear on your message.

You might need to go through several takes before it becomes clear, but keep in mind that the more clear you get on your message, the more people will understand what you do. Speaking legend John Childers often says, "A confused mind never buys." If you are confusing people with your message, how can you expect them to buy? Imagine a lemonade stand that sells only beer. You'll annoy (and not get purchases from) people who wanted lemonade, and will miss (and not get purchases from) people who wanted beer.

When you are clear on your message, you will attract people to you. Imagine not having to work as hard to get people interested in you because your message is so clear that they jump right on it. What would that be like? Imagine the glory of answering phone calls instead of making them. Imagine receiving an email every couple minutes with a sale because people love what you have so much that they're buying it and you're not even doing anything to make it happen.

Imagine putting on a seminar or webinar and when it's over you've made tens of thousands of dollars because you targeted the people willing and able to purchase what you are selling. This, my friend, is why it's extremely important to be clear on your messaging.

This is why it's so important for you to sit down and figure out your exact ideal client.

Create Your "Ideal Client" Template

What I'd like you to do, on the last page in this chapter, is to write out every detail about your ideal client. Ideally, this should be based off of somebody you already know that you would actually want to work with. Remember my example about Amanda? "Amanda" is the model for my ideal client. I know several things about "Amanda." For example, she is married and has two young boys. She is an avid runner. She loves to go to Disneyland. She loves to eat. She loves spending time with her friends and family. She buys new running shoes all the time. She collects race medals. She loves to laugh. She owns a bookkeeping business. You get the point. I know a lot of things about Amanda and I can now advertise to her knowing those specifics about her.

What's cool about this exercise is that when completed you can do all of your marketing and messaging to your "Amanda." Having your ideal client clearly in focus, you will be more effective in creating your marketing materials, when you write a blog article, when you create a video, when you get interviewed by a local TV station, or any other type of marketing materials you put together.

What happens is that you end up speaking to that one person, that ideal client. Just imagine that he or she is on the other side of that camera and you're speaking to him or her, or that he or she is reading your website or business flyer. No longer are you talking to "anybody with skin," but to a real person. Imagine yourself talking to your "Amanda" and having a one-on-one conversation; it's much more natural because you're speaking to one person and it will be an infinitely more compelling sales pitch.

Here's an example. I might do a video talking about running, maybe the fact that I signed up for an upcoming charity 5k run. Now I can do that because I am a runner, too, and thus "Amanda" and I already have a common interest. Same would be true if I were going to Disneyland and I did a video about Disneyland. Amanda would see that video and would be interested because she likes Disneyland. Now she has seen that we have two things in common: Disneyland and running. Because we now have two things in common, she will look at me a little closer when she's looking to buy something. Remember, be YOU!

Once I figured out that Amanda is my ideal client, my ideal clients started finding me. That's called attraction marketing.

Take this information, this ideal client creation exercise, and turn it into a valuable piece of information that you can use in order to discover who you really want to work with, and something you refine over time. It's not just about your ideal client and what her likes and dislikes are, but it's about your own likes and dislikes, attracting clients to you that will make your business life much more enjoyable and profitable. Attract people to you instead of you having to chase people. When you chase people, you actually chase them away. Look at your business and the people you have been serving and try to discover whether you have been chasing after them or you have been attracting them to you. Which is it?

Yes, many people get scared to do this exercise because they feel like if they only pick one person that they won't have any clients, but the opposite is the case. By choosing exactly who it is that you want to work with, it is easier to find them, recognize them, sign them up, and also allow those people to start finding you. If you start filling your client roster with less-than-ideal clients, especially if your business is in the service industry, you will stop having resources to serve your ideal clients when they come along. Yes, sometimes you will get clients who are not squarely within your ideal client mold, but you'll find that those decisions become intentional rather than desperate, and selections that are close enough to your ideal model to be workable.

Remember, your marketing and messaging may be directed to a specific "ideal" person, but there may also be other people who see it and have similar interests. No worries, consider that collateral benefits. For now, don't be scared to outline the qualities you are really looking for in an ideal client.

Get busy figuring out who you want to work with and whose life you want to change with your product or service because they need it and they want it. This will forever change the way you market your services or product.

MY IDEAL CLIENT'S LIKES AND DISLIKES
(ONE PERSON)

_____

_____

_____

_____

_____

_____

_____

_____

_____

_____

_____

_____

_____

Lesson #5 - Treat Time as a Finite Resource

I discovered an important, unfixed law of life during my Year of Fear - even the fearless need a watch. It doesn't matter how fearlessly you approach life, there are still only 24 hours in every day. It's how you use those hours, how you savor their use to further a life well lived, that makes all the difference.

I always thought I had great time management and never considered that I wasn't very good at tracking my time. I've always completed everything I've wanted to complete, so that, naturally, meant that I knew what I was doing with my time and had a good track of it. I worked as a legal secretary for more than 20 years and never missed a deadline. I must be efficient with my time.

Not so much. If I set out for the grocery store a mile down the street at 9am and get home at 5pm with everything on my list of 10 items, that doesn't mean I spent my time wisely.

I hadn't taken the time to identify my goals, what steps it would take to get there, or how to spend my finite resource of time to reach my goals, be they daily or for a lifetime legacy.

Let's be realistic. There are only 24 hours in every day, only seven days in every week, only 12 months in every year, and only some unknown number of years before we are no longer here and can no longer work towards our goals. If we want to meet our goals, we are going to have to have a strategic plan for use of our time.

It wasn't until 2016 at a conference breakout session that I finally realized I was horrible at tracking my time and had extremely poor time management skills. It was also where I learned a great technique for dramatically increasing my time management skills and allowing me to both stay on task and accomplish more in less time.

Set Your Goals

Before you start managing your time, you need to be clear on what you want to accomplish. Like most things in life, having an end result or a goal in mind can help you focus and achieve success. If you don't know what your goal is or what your end result is going to be, then how can you possibly know where to start or what steps to take to get there? Using my grocery store analogy again, if I don't know where the grocery store is or don't have a list of what I need to buy, how will I know if my trip was successful?

Think really hard about what goals you want to set for yourself, not just today or for the next week, but in the big picture of life. When you have these large goals, we'll then work backwards down to the time management of our days.

I recently read John-Leslie Brown's book, *Harvard Effect*, and he recommends creating a 100- year plan. Okay, I agree that might be a little crazy; after all, the odds of any of us living to be 100 years old is very slim. However, if you want to create a legacy, something to leave behind when you're gone, or even when you retire, planning big is crucial.

Imagine leaving behind such a legacy that people behind you are so grateful to you for having done so. What kind of goals do you have that stretch out to your retirement?

For sake of example, let's say that it's another 20 years. Let's say the legacy you want to leave behind is changing the way people use their computers. Maybe in 20 years you see nobody using a computer ever again. Computers are a thing of the past. Computers are in our history and have nothing to do with our future. Computer isn't even a word in the dictionary anymore (except when it refers to history). Maybe that's what you see is your future.

Okay. What do you need to do in the next 20 years in order to make sure you are on track to meet that goal? What would need to happen in the first 10 years? The first five years? The first year?

You will quickly see that the larger goals are more general, whereas at each smaller increment of time, what needs to be done has more specificity. In order for you to know how to get to your big goals, you have to know what smaller steps you are going to take, and the smaller steps beneath that. The idea of goal setting is so that you can know where you are headed so you can create a path to get there.

Now, let me caution you as you embark on this process. Don't get too detailed yet on that stuff this many years away; it will change as you go along anyway. Do have the big picture goals for the longer timeframe, and then for the first few years have more detail?

Using the earlier example about computers being something of the past and only our history, maybe your first step to making that happen is something along the lines of creating a product that will extinguish computers. Since I'm not a computer nerd, I have no idea what that would be, but you probably do. Now that you've thought of the product that you need to create, you need to figure out the steps that you have to take in order to create that product. Then you need to prioritize what you are working on so that you can work smart. Perhaps you first need to obtain funding, then hire research and development staff to help you create a prototype, etc.

Do you see where this is going? Eventually this process of mapping out stepping stones from one thing to another will lead to creation of weekly and daily allocations of your precious resource - time - to accomplish these tasks that, surely and steadily, will get you to your bigger goals. You can make more headway by knowing the step-by-step process of getting there.

You are working on getting from Point A (where you are now) to Point Z (where you want to be in 20 years). The thing is, you can't just step from Point A to Point Z. You have to go from Point A to Point B first, then Point C and so forth. You just need to figure out Points B through Y in more refined detail the closer you get to those points.

Whether 20 years, or 10 years, or five years, or three years, or one year, or six months, or three months, or one month, all of those steps should be tied to, and leading to, your ultimate goal.

Time-Block Your Days

Okay, I get that looking at the next 20 years can be a little intimidating. Spending less time to accomplish more sounds just as intimidating, but let's just break things down into manageable bites (aka bytes).

What I want you to do is create a chart/outline of all the time available to you in any given week. You can do this old-school with a piece of paper with columns for Monday, Tuesday, Wednesday, Thursday, Friday, Saturday and Sunday, or you can create the same chart on a spreadsheet, or you can download my time-blocking chart at www.LivingLive.tv/timeblocking.

For each day, I want you to break it down into half-hour increments. These 336 boxes represent your finite resource of time for the week. First start blocking out time for sleeping, eating, grooming, commuting, etc., leaving you with open time slots to be filled in with work tasks that will move you towards your ultimate goals.

Then start assigning blocks of time to various tasks outlined in your goal-setting exercise, and tasks necessary to run your business. For example, you could block out an hour each Monday morning for writing the weekly blog article for your website, another hour to put posts on your social media accounts, and then two-hour blocks each Tuesday, Wednesday and Thursday for meetings with clients.

This is not always a perfect or clean process. The first time I did the time-blocking I forgot about simple things in life like bathroom breaks, eating, driving from one location to the next, and generally not knowing how long any particular task took. I also found myself double and triple booking time blocks without even realizing it. What time-blocking did, however, was make me stop and be aware of how I was spending my time, making sure that my day's to-do lists would always get done. It helped me gain control of my time. I gained a realistic understanding of time and how long it takes me to do certain tasks. I soon started seeing results of me actually spending less time and accomplishing more.

A side benefit of time-blocking is that it is easier to avoid distractions when you know what you are supposed to be doing during any particular block of time in the day. If you're like a lot of people, including me, you tend to get distracted with what is known as "Squirrel Syndrome" or "Shiny Object Paradox." Do you get distracted easily by things? Do you stop being focused on the things you planned to do because something attractive or interesting popped up on Facebook or in your email box? Something jumps in front of us and, before we know it, we are doing something totally different and are no longer focused on what we were supposed to be working on. Next thing you know, two hours has passed. Squirrel Syndrome makes us get off track and will sidetrack us from that planned process from Point A to Point Z.

Those of us who get off track frequently have a tendency to not accomplish what we need to accomplish in order to become successful. Sometimes our transitory wants want to take a backseat to our needs and goals. If we want success, however, our transitory wants need to take a backseat more frequently. We don't meet our goals because we allowed ourselves to take a path of distraction. I can tell you with firm confidence that most of the failures in my business life were mostly due to my lack of prioritizing my goal-setting plans and time-blocking schedules over the easy distraction of "shiny objects."

What is that very first step that you need to take to get you on the trajectory of reaching Point B? What are the next steps? (See the last page of this chapter for an exercise to help you with this process.)

Once you have a list, it's time to put those steps into more concrete to-do lists and start time-blocking. Time-blocking is one of those things that can really help you gain control of yourself and what you are working on. It also helps you see the realities of time instead of living in a glass bubble like I had been doing for so many decades. If you want to get control of your time and figure out how to spend less time doing more, make this time-blocking technique part of your daily, weekly, and monthly routine.

This exercise should help you get an idea of how much time you actually spend doing tasks. First thing every morning I look at my time-block chart for that day to see what I am going to work on. Then I get started. I set a timer on my phone every 30 minutes. When the alarm goes off, I stop what I'm doing (this was hard at first, but trust me on this), look at my time-block chart to see what my next task is, then I set my timer for 30 minutes and do the next task. After doing this for a couple days it will become easier to break away from what you are working on AND you will start to see progress throughout your day.

Remember, take time to give yourself credit for what you've done and pat yourself on the back every day.

Make More Hours in Your Day With Delegation

The genius of time-blocking is that it also leads you to awareness and planning of delegating tasks to others. If you are like me, you have a hard time delegating. The number one reason people do not like to delegate to other people is because they firmly believe that nobody can do it as good as them. However, as soon as you embrace the beauty of time-blocking you will quickly realize you need more time blocks in every given day and, because time is a finite resource, your only option will be to delegate some of your necessary tasks to others.

If you have a hard time delegating, have no fear, you are in the right place and I'm going to share some secrets with you that are going to help you learn how to delegate, become a great delegator, and enjoy delegating. Delegating is a key element in becoming successful. You can have success singularly all by yourself, and you can have success where you are contributing to the success of the world and the success of others. If you have singular success, guess what? That means you are doing it all by yourself and you are most likely overwhelmed and stressed and feel like you cannot take time off or take a vacation, because if you take time off or take a vacation that means that your business will suffer. I've got news for you. Not only is not delegating bad for you, but it is bad for your clients. If you are under a lot of stress and overwhelmed, then your clients are suffering from not experiencing all the excellence that is within you.

Remember your bold goals and ambitions for the next 20 years? You really want to meet them, but keep running up against the glass door of there being only 24 hours in every day? Then allow yourself to have help accomplishing them by delegating, and thus expanding the number of hours in every day.

The first thing you need to do is discover all the tasks that can be done by somebody else. Time-blocking is the natural vehicle for pointing out these tasks. Look at the 20 hours of work you are trying to cram into your daily schedule and start prioritizing. What things do you enjoy doing? Which things require your unique expertise, and which ones only require generic expertise? Which tasks follow a system or pattern that you've created?

To delegate, you will need to realize that nobody is perfect, but there are people out there that can do your job almost as well as you, and for some tasks, maybe even better than you.

But let's start with baby steps of delegation; I know how hard it is to acknowledge that anyone can help you at all. I heard a saying that 80% good is good enough. If you can resolve yourself to the fact that you can probably find somebody who can do what you do 80% as good as you and you can be fine with that, then it's time for you to find that 80% person.

Let me be clear - this is not an abandonment of your desire to provide only the highest quality services for your clients. This is simply a crutch to get you over the belief that YOU must do everything in order for your business to succeed.

That is simply not true, but you won't feel that way for a while.

Guess what? You might end up finding somebody who is actually better than you. I hate to break the news to you, but there is most likely somebody out there who can do some of the things you do even better than you do. It's impossible for one person to be stellar at every single thing that a business owner needs to do, you included.

Once you have gone through your list of tasks that can be done by somebody else, create your next list of tasks that you actually hate doing. If you hate doing it, then you shouldn't be doing it and that will be your first set of things to delegate. You might say that you like everything that has to do with running a business and you don't want to give up anything, but that is not realistic. Do you really like inputting bills into your accounting program? Filing documents? Taking out the trash? There has to be something you hate doing or are not good at, so don't be embarrassed to delegate those tasks to others. If you keep putting it off, you probably don't want to do it anyway and should delegate it.

Guess what? Rich people delegate.

You might be thinking, "When I'm rich I'll delegate." But the reality is, "You will not become rich if you don't delegate." To be rich, you must think like a rich person. Remember the stories about the lottery winners, athletes and entertainers? If they don't learn how to handle their money when they become rich, they will likely become poor. It's a poor man's mindset that you must get rid of in order to become rich.

Give to Get

If you want to grow as a business, make a larger impact on the world and want to make more money, then you are going to have to give up something. Wouldn't you happily exchange cleaning the office bathrooms for more time spent with paying clients?

Start with one simple thing. Maybe the task you give up is something that only takes one hour a week. Find a virtual assistant that can do that for you. You might have to search for a while to find the right virtual assistant to do that job, but once you have found your virtual assistant that can do that job and do it well, then you can ask that virtual assistant to do one of the other tasks you have on hand.

I was a virtual assistant for 14 years and know how important it is to hire somebody who can do a good job for you. But, if you don't give that person a chance, then you will never grow, and your business will never become the success it can be.

Imagine the perfect assistant for you. Who is that person? Where do they live? What language or languages do they speak? What is their forte? Are they a great speller or are they a great mathematician? Are they a great writer or a great video editor? What skills does that virtual assistant have that you don't want to do anymore or that you keep putting off? Look around your office or your desk and see what has been sitting there for more than one week or two or three weeks. That is the thing that needs to be done by somebody else. You are never going to get to it. How do I know this? Because I know you. You have a lot of aspirations and hopes and dreams that you want to accomplish all these different things because you know you need to accomplish them in order to become successful, but there are only 24 hours in a day and it isn't possible for you to do everything.

The most important trait when delegating is having trust; once trust has been broken, it's hard to get it back. If you have trust in the people you hire to work for you, then they will do a better job for you. Once you start delegating, you must be very clear with the other person what your expectations are. If you are not clear on your expectations, then don't be surprised if the work you get back is not what you wanted. If the work you get back is subpar, instead of firing the person, you may want to give them a chance and see if you can figure out a way to communicate better so that you can tap into their genius and receive the value you want from them.

I recently started looking for a virtual assistant to whom I could delegate some of my work. It was hard at the beginning. I quickly discovered that my communication skills with them were not what they needed. I could easily have blamed them, but chose to learn better how to communicate with them so that I could tap into what they have to offer. We ended up getting on a video conference call and talked about what my needs and wants and desires are for my company and that made them feel like they were part of my team. The work I got back after that was 95% accurate. I was ecstatic about it. Prior to that conversation with them, the work was around 55% accurate. I wasn't happy with that, of course, but once I realized that I was part of the problem (I had to check my ego at the door), it was easy to fix because I was able to get on a call and take care of it right away. We now have a symbiotic relationship and love working with each other.

Delegating is definitely a skill that has to be learned. If you are not accustomed to delegating and having people help you or asking for help, it will take a little while to feel comfortable with it, but you can learn. Don't try to do it alone. Reach out to someone who has hired a virtual assistant and ask them for guidance and help with finding one that will be a good fit for you. It's time for you to start asking for help and discovering to whom you can delegate.

Now, get busy and start time-blocking your days and delegating to increase the amount of time being worked towards your goals, so that you can reach your goals. I want you to imagine yourself one year from now. How much money is your business bringing in? How many staff members do you have working for you? How many clients' lives are you changing? How much of an impact are you making on the earth? Treating your time as a finite resource, and tapping into the time of others, will get you where you want to be.

POINT A (WHERE ARE YOU NOW?)

_____

_____

_____

POINT Z (WHERE DO YOU WANT TO BE?)

_____

_____

_____

POINT B (WHAT IS YOUR FIRST NEXT STEP?)

_____

_____

POINT C (WHAT IS YOUR SECOND NEXT STEP?)

_____

_____

POINT D (WHAT IS YOUR THIRD NEXT STEP (and so on)?)

_____

_____

Lesson #6 - Seek Counsel, Not Opinion

What is Counsel?

When you learn to drive a car, you are taught by an instructor who has learned how to teach you. When you play sports, you have a coach who teaches you how to be the best you can be. They know what you are going through and can guide you along the right path. The same goes with running a successful business. Seek counsel (a sound advisor) who is successfully doing what it is you want to do. They will tell you what to do and what not to do. They will give you advice that could save you time, money and heartache. Been there done that.

What is Opinion?

There is no shortage of opinions out there. Everyone has one. The problem with seeking opinions from people who 1) have no idea what you are working on, 2) have no idea what you are up against, 3) don't know how to run a successful business, 4) don't want to hurt your feelings (the list goes on and on) is that they are not giving you sound advice because they are not savvy to your business. I recommend never asking a friend or family member for business advice (unless they are a successful businessperson who does what you do for your business). They will have your best interest in mind, but they may give you bad advice and that could cause bad feelings.

Finding Someone to Help

I was staring at Facebook one evening, musing as I had been a lot during that period of my life, "there's gotta be more to life" when, out of the blue, there it was, an invitation from a life coach. "I've been a life coach for years and took some time off. I'm coming back to coaching and am looking for 5 women who want to change their life," Liz's post read. The post was in a private Facebook group I belonged to and it piqued my curiosity. Well, it actually did more than that; it sort of smacked me in the face. There it was. The sign I had been looking for. Liz was going to be the one who would change my life.

I immediately contacted her and said, "I'm in" and signed the paperwork. The following several months she guided me through the work of reinventing my life, helping me find within myself that "more to life" I had been looking for. She asked all the right questions (even though I HATED those questions because I didn't really want to dive deep) and she was persistent. She helped me discover more about me than I ever imagined was possible. Those questions unlocked the door to me doing everything I've done since that time. That was August 2014 and I have never turned back.

Had Liz not posted in the private group and had I not seen the post and had I not acted on the post, my life might be the same as it was back then.

Partnering with a coach was the best gift I ever gave myself because it gave me an opportunity to answer questions I would NEVER have asked myself and led me down paths I never would have dared take otherwise.

Shortly after I met my life coach, she and I attended a vision board seminar where attendees assemble a collage of pictures and words depicting what they want in life. A vision board serves as a constant reminder of what you envision for your future by looking at it every day.

I didn't prepare a vision board that day, but, instead, watched the speakers at the event. One of those speakers was a gentleman by the name of Greg Reid. Greg had an eloquent way of speaking and he really kept my attention the entire time he spoke. I truly believe that he was put into this place in my life at the time that I needed him to be there. He shared with us an event he produces called "Secret Knock." I found out how much it cost and immediately believed that I could not afford it. My life coach, however, strongly encouraged me to go and offered to get me a discounted ticket. It still seemed like too much money, but I decided to trust the new positive path I was on and went ahead and put the money down and went. After all, when your life coach tells you to do something, you do it. I was in a huge growth spurt at this time, so I did what she said. Sometimes you just have to have faith, throw caution to the wind and jump in and do whatever it is that is scaring you so you can progress and learn and grow and change and become a better person.

Before I go on to tell you about how amazing a circumstance this event turned out being for me, I would be remiss in not cautioning you about potential scams. As certain high-profile lawsuits have shown, there are a few organizations out there who try to spin your quest for positivity into cash for them with no substance to the program. Be smart and do your homework in advance of paying for any expensive program.

That being said, the "Secret Knock" program turned out to be one of the most amazing events I had ever attended and worth every penny. It helped me understand and solidify my quest for positivity in my life.

One of the things that Greg said during his talk that really stuck out to me was to seek counsel, not opinion. The reason that stuck out so much is because I had spent most of my life asking for people's opinions instead of asking people who were where I wanted to be, people who actually had knowledge of value. I discovered the reason I asked for opinion instead of counsel is because I was too scared of what the responses might be if I had asked somebody smarter than me. If you ask for an opinion, they may say something nice just to be polite. That's kind, but not helpful if you are trying to grow personally or professionally. It's not that I thought I was the smartest person around, but I definitely didn't want to feel like I was the dumbest person in the room (and, as we already established earlier, I can be kind of pigheaded in the face of helpful advice).

Reading what I just wrote, I realize how dumb it was of me not to want to look dumb for so many years. The smartest people are the ones who are willing to ask questions, all the time, and asking questions doesn't really make you look dumb after all. Even if it occasionally does, so what? I'll look a little dumb in the short term if the result is me learning more and becoming smarter in the long run.

Those four simple words changed so much of my life. Seek counsel, not opinion. Seek counsel from people who know more than you do.

Another thing I learned through these events was to realize that I am so much better than I ever gave myself credit for.

It was time for me to start living my life as the person I am. But, first, I had to discover who that was and I needed expert help to sort those things out.

The path to discovering the excellence that I have within me was an amazing journey (that I'm still on and hope to be on until my last breath). I highly recommend that if you want to live a better life, you reach out to somebody who is where you want to be. Get guidance from others who can see you better than you see yourself, and let them guide you to a reawakening of your inherent talents.

The same applies to more mundane, but no less important, aspects of your business. Are you unfamiliar with keeping financial books? Connect with a good bookkeeper and CPA. Don't know how to market your business? Find someone to do it for you, or teach you how.

When you are looking for counsel to help you become the person you want to become or have the business that you want to run, reach out to somebody who is actually doing what you want to do and is successful doing that. Continue this process throughout your business and the accumulated knowledge and insight will dramatically increase your business success.

Lesson #7 - Surround Yourself With Positive Energy

Fear in life is often situational. When you surround yourself with the right people and the right energy, fears become smaller and far more conquerable.

It was 6:00 in the morning and I was on the freeway heading for work. The traffic was so thick, unbearable and slow that I was getting angry. Looking back, I can't believe I said the things I said at that time, but, at that time in my life, the darkness I was living in, anger was a common and daily experience. As I was driving, I exclaimed loudly to myself, "There better be someone hurt up there. I'm going to be late." Instead of chiding myself for leaving later than I should have, I was not only blaming somebody else for my delay, but hoping they had been punished for it. I'm ashamed to say it today, but that was the way I lived my life on a daily basis. There was always somebody else to blame for my faults. Truth is, I should have left for work earlier. I knew it was raining and I knew that when it rains traffic backs up. It was my fault for leaving too late, certainly not the fault of someone else who might at that very moment be bleeding and headed for an emergency room. It's a startling reality, but I now realize how my negativity brought negativity to me.

The Law of Attraction brings back to you what you put out there, and not just the positive stuff. I was putting out a lot of negative thoughts and negative thoughts were finding their way back to me. Not only were negative thoughts finding their way back to me, but negative people were finding their way to me, too.

Probably the primary source of my negativity was feeling unsupported by others; everything else grew out of that. Was I really unsupported? Or did I just feel like I was unsupported? I don't know the real answer, because that's not really what is important. What I thought was the reality, became my actual reality. Whatever we feel is our reality is our reality. We feel what we feel, and even if it isn't "real" to begin with, it soon becomes real.

When you surround yourself with negative people who don't support you, you tend to drift off into the darkness and don't feel motivated to do much. It leaves you with loneliness and negativity yourself. I was surrounded by negative people and I was negative. It took me years and years before I emerged from that darkness and discovered who I really am, but you don't have to wait that long. You can learn today what took me years to learn. Who I am today makes me realize how important it is to embrace my initial motivating forces, and then surround myself with supportive people who are positive, uplifting, and powerful.

Identify What Motivates You

How do you keep yourself motivated to keep going and keep doing what it is that you want to accomplish? This is a question I get frequently because I have now reached a point where I am very self-motivated and task-motivated. Once I know what goals I have set and how much time it is going to take, I set my wheels in motion to accomplish the task so that I can be successful.

It wasn't always like this for me, though. Back in the old days, before I started deliberate goal-setting and time-blocking, my mind was all over the place and I was a wreck. Once I started tracking my time I started to see how much of it was wasted and how much of it was used effectively. I realized that I actually love using my time effectively and I crave success more than screwing off and not getting stuff done. So I kind of made a game for myself of motivation; I pat myself on the back as often as I possibly can. It's a fun way for me to see what I've accomplished and gives me a perspective of how far I have come. It allows me to gloat about how awesome I am (well, to myself - which is a healthy thing, by the way).

I believe that too often we don't give ourselves credit for how amazing we are. I know you are amazing because you are reading this book; you are purposefully seeking knowledge and assistance in living a fearless entrepreneurial life. If you weren't amazing and didn't want to know how to become a good new entrepreneur, you wouldn't be reading this book. You can motivate yourself in the same manner I have.

What is your motivating factor that keeps you going so that you can live the life you want, to live with whom you want, to live it where you want, and how you want to live it? Something made you pick up this book, something made you become an entrepreneur. You wanted to contribute something to this world. That is what should motivate you to keep moving forward and to keep making progress so that you can live that life you want.

Carefully Select the People in Your Life

The subject of positive people is a very interesting subject and, believe it or not, it can be subjective. A person who is positive to you might appear to be a negative person to somebody else. This is all your perspective. Your perspective is grounded in your history and your present. Select the people around you with care, looking for people who make you a better person for being around them. Once you start living around positive people who make you feel good about yourself, you will notice the change in who you are. Imperceptibly, you will become positive and supportive just like they are. And vice versa. If you are the person who is positive and uplifting and people start seeing you for who you are, then you will start being one of those positive people that others seek out for a positive influence in their lives. It's all a matter of reversing the prior course of negative people attracting negative people. However, once you feel comfortable in this space, I urge you to find a new environment of positive people so you can continue to grow.

When I was critical and judgmental of people, there were probably some positive people in my life, but I didn't see them. I do remember a few times, probably more than a few, when somebody would say something that was positive and I just looked at them like they didn't know what they were talking about. Little did I know, they knew more about what they were talking about than I had even an inkling about. They had made the discovery of positivity long before I had.

When I started discovering positivity and how it could change my life, I wanted everyone around me to drink the elixir I had, I wanted them to see the same light I had and become a positive person and totally change their life. I wanted everyone to discover what I had discovered, the simple discovery that when you surround yourself with positive people you will become a positive person. And when you become a positive person, you can positively impact other people's lives.

Law of Attraction

I have been fortunate to be able to continue to share these lessons with others. Amanda, the client I referenced before, has done incredibly well and has increased her income by so much, just by changing her mindset and surrounding herself with positive influences. Her mindset didn't change overnight; it was a process. But once it changed, once she opened her mind to the possibilities around her, her entire life changed. This is something that she will have for the rest of her life. No longer on government aid, being able to take her sons to summer camp, being able to get her hair done more frequently, being able to buy that Starbucks coffee that she likes, etc. She chose positivity, and positivity has cycled back around to bless her. This is a classic example of the Law of Attraction at work. In short, the Law of Attraction is defined as, "Whatever you put out into the universe, you attract back to you - be it negative or positive."

Sometimes the transition into a positive lifestyle comes through sheer power of will, despite apparent obstacles. I have certainly pushed the boundaries of that. It's hard to be on a quest for positivity without also deciding to spend the rest of your life having as much fun as you can being surrounded by positive and uplifting people who want to make a change in the world. That's exactly the quest I have been on, and that is exactly what I've been finding.

When you put out to the universe what you want, it finds you. At that point, I hadn't even heard about the Law of

Attraction, but I discovered that when I wanted to find something, I needed to put out there what I wanted and then it would eventually find me.

You may start noticing the Law of Attraction at work in subtle ways throughout your workweek. For example, the other day I was on a conference call and we were talking about having a specific colleague, John, help us with what we were working on. After I got off the conference call and before I had done anything to contact John, there was an email in my inbox from John asking me if there was anything I needed help with. It was so odd, but I realized that it was because we had "put it out there" during the call.

It is also amazing what can happen if you share what your hopes and dreams are with others. That's actually what a vision board is all about. Yes, I finally completed one. The concept is to put your ideas out there of what you want your life to be and then the universe will send it to you. If you put out a bunch of negativity, having a nightmare board if you will, then negativity will find you.

Once you start changing your mindset and start surrounding yourself with positive people, your entire world will change. It might feel awkward for you at the beginning if you're not used to that, but stick with it and you will find that it becomes your new normal. A new normal sometimes comes with amazing surprises.

A few years ago I would never have imagined myself being in the same room as the inventor of the magnetic strip on the back of the credit & debit card, or a co-founder of the Make-A-Wish Foundation, or the creator of Ugg boots, founder of Chuck E. Cheese, or the guy the hit TV show Scorpion was created after, or Olympic gold medalists. That's just a small example of some of the people I have met during my path of surrounding myself with positive and uplifting people. These people are amazing and one of the things I absolutely love about these entrepreneurial spirits is that they "get me." They totally understand what I'm going through and who I am and they want nothing more than to help me on my path to becoming successful. They believe in cooperation and collaboration, not competition. They are here to serve and serve as many people as possible.

Find Supportive People Who "Get You"

You may be married or have siblings or parents or other people in your life who don't really understand why you want to do what you want to do. That's okay; you cannot pick your family. They don't understand it because they don't "get you." In order for people to "get you," they have to be like you and sometimes it takes a little work to find them.

Did you know that Thomas Edison was expelled from school for being too dumb? He was a very young boy and the teacher sent him home with a note telling his mother that she needed to keep him at home because he was too dumb for the school. Well, his mother, being brilliant in her own right, turned that negativity into a positive. Instead of telling Thomas that he was sent home because he was too dumb, she told him that he was sent home from school because he was too smart for the school and that nobody could teach him except for her. So she home-schooled him. I, for one, am grateful that his mother was smart enough and kind enough to encourage her son to be all that he could be. She had that rare foresight to tell her son how amazing he was. The teacher was not supportive and did not "get" Thomas Edison. His ideas, even as a young boy, were so out of the box that the teacher didn't understand it.

What happens with a lot of entrepreneurs is exactly that. People don't understand us because we don't think like they think we're supposed to. We think outside of the box, and that is the brilliance of our minds. Entrepreneurs are the ones who have created everything you're looking at right now. Whether you are reading this book on your phone or computer or listening to it on audio or sitting down with a book in your lap and reading it, whatever you're looking at right now was created by an entrepreneur who saw something possible that others did not.

As happened with Thomas Edison, entrepreneurs who think outside of the box of traditional ideas are often misunderstood by others around them. Sometimes we can get shot down by people who just don't get us, and we shut ourselves down and distrust our instincts. That's what happened to me when I was young.

I was told on a daily basis for two years that I was stupid and I would never amount to anything. My 8th grade geometry teacher told me that I was stupid and that I should not continue with math. My 8th grade geometry teacher was likewise unsupportive. My teacher's words stuck with me for quite a while, but in 10th grade I decided to take math again. Actually, I didn't have a choice, because math was a requirement for graduating high school, but I also used it as my opportunity to take back my dignity and intellect. I ended up getting A's in all of my math classes after that and even ended up successfully working at a bank as a supervisor after graduating high school.

Until we are able to surround ourselves with the right people, there will be some people who don't support us and don't understand what we are going through, and sometimes even feel the need to knock us down. It is up to us to pick ourselves back up.

What if you were surrounded by positive and supportive and uplifting people who wanted nothing more than to see you succeed? What would that be like? Well, I can tell you exactly what it's like for me because that is who I'm surrounded by on a daily basis now. Those other people, the non-supportive types, are a thing of my past and they don't shape my future in any way, shape, or form. Being surrounded by positive and uplifting people gives me this feeling of euphoria, a feeling that everything I do is done for the right reason and the right purpose.

It's so amazing because their positive outlook and their encouragement gives me a reason to keep going and to keep doing what it is that I am doing. Being with positive people doesn't mean they always agree with you, but means they support and uplift you. Even when they don't agree with you, they will give you advice that can propel you to the next level. Rather than try to break your spirit, let your ego take a hike and listen to their advice.

You've discovered your purpose of why you are here and now it's time for you to take that and do something with it. It's not impossible to do when you're surrounded by negative people, but it sure is a lot easier to do when you're surrounded by positive people. Find people in your life who make you feel good when you are around them and those who make you want to keep going and do more. Those are the people you need to surround yourself with as often as possible. Here's how you do it.

Do an inventory of the people in your life. Use the last page of this chapter to write the names of all the positive people in your life. If you feel good when you are with them and feel uplifted when you leave them, write their name. Then list people you WANT to be around. With the Law of Attraction at work, this can come to fruition. Let's say, for example, you are surrounded by positive people 1 hour every day of the week. The other 23 hours of every day you are surrounded by negative people. You can shift this balance slowly; it doesn't have to be quick. For example, from this point forward make it a point to spend an extra half hour every day with positive people. What I mean by this is that if you are currently surrounded by positive people 1 hour every day, next week I want you to surround yourself with positive people 1 1/2 hours every day. The following week I want you to surround yourself with positive people 2 hours every day, then 2 1/2 hours, and so on. This can take different forms, like changing your clientele, changing who your co-workers are, changing the place where you work, or making changes in the amount of time you spend with family and friends.

Trust me, this will work. It worked for me and it will work for you, too. You will see a shift happen in your life that will be scary at times because it won't make sense to you and the life you have been living, but it will turn into something that's going to be your daily life. Trust and have faith in the process.

I remember when I first started on this journey and I was about four or five months into it. Things were so amazing and my whole body and brain were surrounded by positivity and I felt like I was floating on air. It was so incredible that I remember specifically one day saying out loud to myself, "When is this going to end?" The reason I thought that was because I had never had anything in my life that was like this. At least not for this long. It had become like being on vacation, having a great time, but counting down in your mind the days and hours until the vacation was over. These days, however, it doesn't end.

Once I discovered who I am and who I want to be and started living my life authentically, everything started changing and started becoming a daily life of bliss. Part of this journey of becoming authentic was learning who the supportive and positive people are and then becoming a positive and supportive person myself.

Stop Judging and Start Supporting

Once I started becoming a positive and supportive person, I found that I stopped judging people. The two things went hand-in-hand. I observed this and tried to discover why this was the case and I have a theory. I believe it's because once you start concentrating on yourself and growing as a person, you don't see the badness in other people. It's still there, but you just don't see it because you are busy with other things.

THE YEAR OF FEARS

It was about one year into my journey when I realized that I was no longer judging people for the things I had previously been judging them about. It was quite an amazing epiphany. I would see a lady walking down the street who looked very fancy and looked like she was all that, and looked at her in a totally different light than I had just one year earlier. Instead of seeing her as somebody who was stuck up (which was what I previously thought), I saw her as someone who was confident, maybe somebody I could look up to for that quality; maybe I could learn from her. Once I started seeing positive and confident people as people I could potentially learn from, it really started changing me even more. It put me on a faster track to becoming a more positive and uplifting person myself. Once I started becoming more positive and uplifting, I was able to impact more people's lives in a positive way. This became my mission, to impact positively as many lives as possible. My goal is to positively impact 5.5 million people during my lifetime. I'm starting off small, but I have my 20-year plan and the means of executing it!

Supporting people is something I strive to do on a daily basis. It's very simple to do. You just have to set your mind to it and do it. Ask people "How can I support you?" When you surround yourself with positive people, most of the time you will find that they actually have a response to that question. They are people who have discovered who they are, what they want, and understand that they will need others to help them along their way. When you know what you want, you know what kind of support you need. Reach out to those people in your life who are positive and especially reach out to those who are where you want to be in life. Those people will tell you things you need to do in order to get there.

Believe it or not, most successful people believe in collaboration and cooperation, not competition. It's usually the people who are on the bottom rung of some corporate ladder who are competing with each other to get to the top. Those who are on the top have little reason to worry about their competition. They also know that there is an abundance of money to be had and that there is no reason why it can't be shared with others. Therefore, you will find that the most successful people also are the most accessible people.

I have certainly found this to be the case. Every time I have reached out to somebody I thought might be inaccessible, I was surprised to find that they were accessible. Not only were they accessible, but they wanted to help me. Generally, the most successful people are the most supportive people. There are many examples of this. Think about Bill Gates, Richard Branson, Oprah Winfrey, and, of course, Ellen DeGeneres, some highly successful people who are also known for supporting and encouraging others. These people make it their mission to be supportive and help as many people as they possibly can. They are at the top and love supporting others.

Think about it. What is something that you want to do and are putting off? Are you putting it off because you don't know what to do? If that is the case, then reach out to somebody to ask for support. Build that circle of positivity around you. You might be pleasantly surprised to find out that when you ask for help from people who are ahead of you that they are much more likely to help you than you imagine.

POSITIVE PEOPLE I LOVE BEING AROUND

_____

_____

_____

_____

_____

_____

POSITIVE PEOPLE I WANT TO BE AROUND

_____

_____

_____

_____

_____

_____

_____

Getting Started

It's possible after reading this book you still have some doubts about being an entrepreneur. That's okay. Many of us have doubts about what we are doing or why we are doing it. Figure out who you are, start living your life authentically, start putting yourself out there and make the difference that you are here to make.

Give yourself the time and space to figure it out. Maybe even embark on your own Year of Fears as I did. Creation, and change, often happen during silence, away from the noise of the world. Even when you are asleep, your brain is still thinking. Isn't that cool? That's one of the reasons why it is good to read something before you go to bed. Your brain will think about it and many times your brain will find a solution for you while you are asleep.

I know a billionaire who does something he calls info-sponging. It's a really cool process. He will read something about one industry, for example the shipping industry, and he'll find something that interests him about that and read about it. The next day he will read something about a different industry that has nothing to do with the shipping industry, for example surfboards, and then when he goes to sleep he will think about both industries and ask his brain, "How can I use these two industries together and create a product or service that can combine the two industries?" It doesn't work for everything, but he has actually invented some really amazing products due to his info-sponging. It's worth a try for the rest of us, too. Before you go to bed, make sure you fill your brain with questions that it can answer while you are sleeping.

Have you ever awakened in the middle of the night with "the answer" to the question you had? I have. It is so exciting to be able to wake up and have the answer to the question you had been asking yourself. Take this information and use it.

I strongly believe that every single person was placed on earth to fulfill a purpose. Some of us are led astray and never make our way back, yet some are led astray and find their way back. If you are just now starting your journey, this is the perfect time to develop good habits, the habits of fearless entrepreneurs. Let me help you get started: www.livinglive.tv/startnow.

Your life starts right now. Your time is right now. Don't let any more time go by without living the life you were meant to live and spending the time with the people you are meant to spend your time with. Start now.

Staying Connected

I'd love to hear from you. What fears have you had that you've confronted and kicked to the curb? What fears are you still working on? What fears have you not yet addressed?

I love receiving emails with stories from people telling me how they've confronted their fears, so send an email to me at Lynda@LivingLive.tv

Download my free Live Video Content Planner if you're interested in learning how to break through your fear of doing live videos: www.LivingLive.tv/vcp

Schedule a discovery call to see how I can help you work through some of your fears to put you on the path to freedom: www.LivingLive.tv/30

I look forward to hearing from you.

Lynda M West

If you are not Living Live, you are not Living.

p.s. Did I ever tell you about the time I ran away when I was 5 years old and was gone a whole week? Yeah, that's a whole other story.

www.ingramcontent.com/pod-product-compliance
Lightning Source LLC
Chambersburg PA
CBHW071222220526

45468CB00002B/699